Mandala Design Coloring

Copyright: Published in the United States Peter Raymond
Published April 2016
ISBN-13: 978-1530904976
ISBN-10: 1530904978

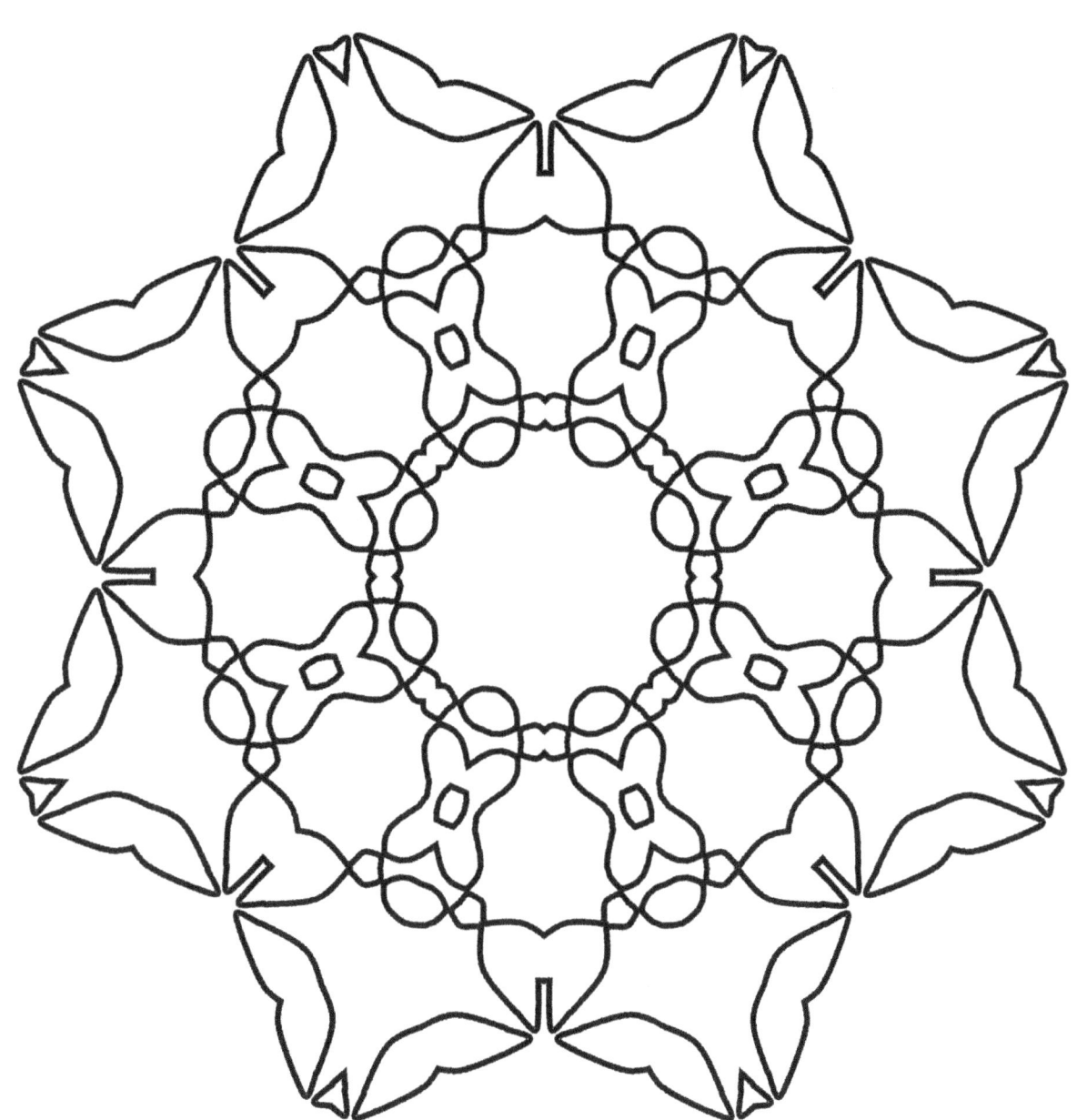

Thank you

www.ingramcontent.com/pod-product-compliance
Lightning Source LLC
Chambersburg PA
CBHW081555280526
45788CB00011B/3478